This book may be kept

The Manager: A Profile

The Manager: A Profile

Richard C. Anderson
and staff of the
Creative Management Center

Correlan Publications
California
1972

Other books by Richard C. Anderson:
Management Practices
Management Strategies

For information address
Correlan Publications
17259 Clearview Drive
Los Gatos, California 95030

Library of Congress Catalog Card Number 72-7667

Manufactured in the United States of
America

38,695

Preface

This book is one of a series prepared by the Creative Management Center for the practicing manager. These books, written by managers experienced in a wide range of activities and industries, combine basic managerial concepts with practical operating methods.

The thesis of the Center's books is that the manager's success is determined by the way he organizes the work of his enterprise and by the extent to which he stimulates people to employ their talents in productive effort. Each book in the series deals with a single aspect of the manager's job, providing a comprehensive and concentrated discussion of that aspect.

The Manager: A Profile describes the effective manager, emphasizing the qualities of attitude and skill that lead to success in management. It provides an overview of managerial practice, touching on various methods and techniques that managers have found will yield positive results. The basic practices referred to here are dealt with more completely in other books of the Center's series.

The profile of the manager as drawn here is not a description of personality traits. Rather, it is a chronicle of behavioral patterns and practices that can be learned.

A word about the illustrations. The line drawings depict managers in various settings, emphasizing the dynamic character of the manager's job. The medallions are taken from the symbolism used by various cultures and societies to portray in artistic form the essential elements of their beliefs. The symbols selected for this book depict two fundamental principles that lie at the center of managerial practice: *first,* systematic and organized patterns built around basic designs and structures; and *second,* the creative and dynamic relationships between human beings.

Table of Contents

The Manager: A Profile

Who is wise? He who learns from all men.
Who is strong? He who controls his passions.
Who is rich? He who is happy with his lot.
Who is honored? He who honors his fellow men.

Are managers a breed apart? Is the managerial profession really different from other occupations?

As with most such questions, the answer is yes and no.

The manager is the same human being with the same emotions, the same prejudices, and the same intellectual processes. He does, however, have a unique set of tasks, and you as a manager do employ a number of skills in ways quite different from those required in other occupations. From the developing body of knowledge on management practice, it is clear that successful managers possess certain distinct attributes and skills. This book concerns those attributes and skills.

The question is often asked, "Are leaders born and not made?"

There is no doubt that success in management as in any other endeavor rests in part upon qualities you were born with, and perhaps someone with more inherited ability will beat you to the finish line. It is abundantly clear, however, that top honors go to those who work for it.

Before we get into a consideration of managerial traits, we should ask, "What is this job we call management?"

The term "manager" as we use it here refers to that person whose primary duty is to guide the affairs of other people. He may be the president of a vast industrial empire, a foreman on the canning line of a food processing plant, an administrator in a school system, or a chief clerk in an Internal Revenue office. Wherever he is, his work product is the released energy of people, and his performance is measured by the accomplishments of other people.

In the following discussion you will see how certain attributes and skills have been used effectively by successful managers. These are attributes and skills that can be learned. They are not inherent traits of personality.

The qualities that make for success in management are discussed from two points of view:

First, *attributes* of behavior
Second, *skills* of practice

No great significance is attached to the distinction between attributes and skills, for in some instances the two are difficult to separate. The distinction does help, however, to show that the one (attributes) is a matter of personal attitude whereas the other (skill) manifests itself in some form of action.

In considering *attributes* we should distinguish between the attributes of *personality* and those of *behavior*. To tell you that as a manager you must have integrity, honesty, loyalty, or other such honorable qualities doesn't help you very much. In the first place, how do you learn honesty and integrity? Even if these traits could be identified and even agreeing that they are important in management, they are no less important in any other occupation.

We may someday have sufficient knowledge of human personality to understand the significance of personality traits and how to identify them. Despite the popular cliches and caricatures, however, all existing evidence suggests that there are no "managerial" personalities. To the contrary, many different types of personalities

have been effective in management. On the other hand, there is substantial evidence that certain types of *behavior* and certain *practices* generate productivity and that certain others interfere with such results.

While the attributes and skills discussed below are important for success in management, seldom will you find all these characteristics in one person. The most that can be said is that effective managers have a number of these attributes and skills and that the more of them you can develop in yourself, the more favorable will be the odds for success.

Attributes

The attributes of behavior are the learned patterns of attitude and demeanor. As you develop these attributes, you will find yourself creating the type of environment in which people identify their interests with those of the enterprise. Such an identity is absolutely essential to the stability and productivity of your endeavor.

Commitment

The committed individual says, "If it is necessary, it is possible." The late Vince Lombardi expressed it this way, "I never lost a game, but once in awhile time ran out on us."

The effective performer, by his single-minded determination, displays a tenacious staying power. He sets an example for others. His aim is to see that his efforts and the efforts of others yield a tangible result.

Woodrow Wilson, speaking of Robert E. Lee, described this quality: "When you come into the presence of a leader of men, you know you have come into the presence of fire—that it is best not uncautiously to touch that man and that there is something that makes it dangerous to cross him."

More humorously, it has been said that every organization has four kinds of people:

1. The wish-bones who spend all their time wishing someone else would do the job.
2. The jaw-bones who do all the talking but nothing else.
3. The knuckle-bones who knock everything that is done by someone else.
4. The back-bones who get things done.

If you are satisfied with what you are doing and if you enjoy seeing it done in the best possible way, you could be described as committed to your work. If not, you should ask yourself these questions:

1. Do I really enjoy myself only when pursuing my hobbies?
2. Do I put in extra hours on my job only because I have to or because I'll get paid overtime for it?
3. Are my week-ends and vacations the only pleasures that I have to look forward to? (You wouldn't be normal if you did not daydream about that mountain stream or waves breaking on the open beach once in awhile.)
4. Do my associates stimulate me, or do they bore me?
5. Do I try to find ways to do my job better and to improve the situation for others?

There is plenty of routine and more than enough boredom in even the ideal job; but if your job does not give you the type of satisfaction implied by these questions, it may be time to reexamine your occupation. You

"When you come into the presence of a leader of men, you know you have come into the presence of fire—that it is best not uncautiously to touch that man and that there is something that makes it dangerous to cross him."
Woodrow Wilson

have either an unrealistic aspiration in your work, or you are in the wrong occupation. Look at the characteristics of a managerial job described in the following pages and see if these are the types of challenges that stimulate you.

Perception

"What a man does not work out for himself, he does not have." One of the most inspiring phrases in the English language is Shakespeare's famous line, "To thine ownself be true." The better you know yourself, the better you can interpret what you see in others and relate constructively to them.

Since not all men are motivated by the same drives, your success in stimulating people will depend on your ability to recognize the unique differences in individual motivation:

- Is this person driven by money above all else?
- Does he have a great pride in status?
- Does he seek primarily intellectual challenge?

Whatever the individual motivation, your effort should be to stimulate each individual within his own image, drives, and goals.

Here are some tested methods you can use to appraise the skills, interests, and objectives of others:

1. How does he perform his tasks? Is he systematic and organized; does he have an analytical approach to his work; is he compulsive or impulsive; does he move rapidly or deliberately; does he work best in groups or in solitude; is he congenial or aloof?

2. Does he have a bent for any particular type of task? Does he prefer the creative to the routine; is he skilled

in the use of numbers; does he function best in people-to-people relationships; does he have mechanical or electronic aptitudes; or does he shine when given a knotty administrative problem?

3. Has he expressed interest in particular occupations through personally initiated education or training?

4. What talents do his fellow workers recognize in him?

5. What objectives and goals has he set for himself? Does he know where he wants to be or what he wants to do five or ten years from now?

"Every man is entitled to the defects of his virtues."
Supreme Court Justice Oliver Wendell Holmes

Your knowledge of these aspects will greatly enhance your capability to organize and direct the affairs of your organization and to motivate people to outstanding performance.

One of the greatest weaknesses in any society is the gulf that separates the leader from the people. Only when the manager has established rapport with his group can that group develop its optimum potential. Just as the sales manager must know when his salesmen are "cold" on an item in the product line, so you as a manager should know if your programs are being undermined by lukewarm support from the rank and file.

After a gruelling meeting in which George Ball, a major figure in the Johnson administration, strenuously opposed expanding the Vietnam war, President Johnson said to him, "George, I can't tell you how grateful I am to you for disagreeing with me." Every experienced manager can understand the President's feelings, for he realizes that he must somehow discern the true thoughts and attitudes of his associates. When you know where your associates stand, you will know what results to expect.

in modern management practice—some of it even in the sugar-coated employee "benefits" programs.

To emphasize human values does not mean to neglect the need for sound business results. On the contrary, a concentration on the human element strengthens economic results by expanding each member's contribution to the economic whole. This broader view rejects the narrow concentration on immediate dollars at the expense of human motivation and productivity.

Concern for the human element does not ignore financial realities. On the contrary, by opening broader avenues for human performance, a greater economic return is achieved.

One of the most serious barriers to achieving an atmosphere of human well-being is the combative attitude of managers who look upon their associates as opponents on a field of battle. In such an atmosphere, survival means striking the first blow out of the conviction that to do otherwise is to perish. To the crafty and cunning, this is a fascinating game, but for the victims—and they constitute the majority of the group—it is a perilous existence.

You have it in your control to choose your own method: cooperation or combat. The overwhelming burden of evidence shows that the former is by far the most productive course.

The manager occupies a unique place in human enterprise. In the process of reaching his goal of group productivity, it is to his advantage to see that each member of the group achieves something for himself, too. If his objective is to manipulate others to gratify his own sense of power, he can always find servile people willing to oblige. When he succumbs to this temptation, however, he impairs his ability to bring out the best in other

. . . a concentration on the human element strengthens economic results by expanding each member's contribution to the economic whole.

people—which in the long run is the only way he can realize the full potential of his organization.

A man motivated solely by the desire for mastery over others can never be their master. But when men know their leader is "for them", they are for him—whatever the consequences. The result is a team effort that can outperform any group dominated by an autocratic leader.

To be compassionate means to understand the human condition and to accept man as he is—with all his strengths and all his frailties. Supreme Court Justice Oliver Wendell Holmes said, "Every man is entitled to the defects of his virtues." Holmes' perceptive observation of human character is wise counsel for the manager. People's talents come in all shapes and sizes, and some of us have more strengths (or weaknesses) than others. The wise manager makes the best use of them all.

Given a normal complement of aptitudes, what a person does with his life is much more dependent on his opportunities and his challenges than on his native talents. As a manager, it is your privilege to help each person bring to full flower those talents that are his alone. As you learn to accommodate others' idiosyncracies, you can expect them to tolerate yours.

If you allow yourself to lose faith in people or to be discouraged when let down by someone's shortcoming, you will be forever discouraged and disillusioned. What you need here is the perspective of the psychiatrist who said to his kleptomaniac patient, "You'll never have a desire to steal again; but if you do have a relapse, try to get me a portable TV, will you?"

A man motivated solely by the desire for mastery over others can never be their master.

Respect

The basis for a sound and constructive business relationship is a mutual acceptance of each others' prerogatives. This means your respect for others and others' respect for you. You know when you respect someone else; but from your managerial position, it is more difficult for you to distinguish between deference and respect. They are not the same thing. Deference entails a regard for the position or status of another. Respect, on the other hand, rests upon acceptance of the person for what he is.

Respect entails a recognition that while some people may have a greater *impact* on the organization because of their responsibility or ability, every person is *important*. The philosopher Rabelais said, "So much is a man worth as he esteems himself." By showing that you respect each person for what he is, you fortify his feeling of self-esteem and stimulate his productive effort.

When you demonstrate that you are sincerely ready to hear people out, you show your respect for their views. You may, like Disraeli, say, "I listen, I agree, and sometimes I forget." Your position may change as new evidence unfolds; but when you consider what another has to say, you strengthen his self-esteem. It was said of Franklin Roosevelt that when listening to your story, he made you feel that your ideas were the most important thing in the world to him at that moment. If people can say this of you, they know they can expect a fair hearing.

To get someone else to agree with you is pleasant, but more pleasant still is the knowledge that something will happen as a result of what you say. When *you* act on the suggestion of another, let him know it. Equally important, tell other people where the idea came from.

14

The wisdom of the young man recently married has meaning for the manager: "I am not going to appropriate her ego just because I love her." You do not "own" the people working with you. When you encourage people to develop their own talents, you build a broad base of productive effort from each person's own motivation.

Forthrightness

One of the saddest tasks faced by any manager is the termination of an unsatisfactory employee. However distasteful the job, the "firing" of an employee is sometimes unavoidable. To put off the dreary duty when it is obviously inevitable serves only to impair confidence in management's judgment and to prolong the employee's distress.

If a person's performance is unsatisfactory, he usually knows it well enough himself—if you have always been honest with him about his work. To help such an employee face the situation squarely is the only prudent course for you and the only fair course for him. Whether the decision be pleasant or unpleasant, when events demand action, the sooner that action is taken, the better for all concerned.

The effective manager is not intimidated by the impact of his act. He does what he believes to be right. He looks for the best course then acts without hesitation. He takes the consequences with good grace if things do not turn out for the best. Or—and this takes courage—when things start to turn sour, he admits his error and changes his course. Acting in good conscience, he is willing to "take the rap" for his decision.

When you look for alternative courses available to you, on rare occasions one stands out clearly as the only possible solution. In most situations there will be more

. . . the will to achieve is nine-tenths the achieving.

than one reasonable answer. At this point, you should ask yourself, Is it necessary to act at all? If you wait, the problem may go away. It is amazing how many problems dissolve if you leave them alone. But you can't afford to count on this to bail you out of your dilemma very often.

Assuming you have found it necessary to choose one course from among several, your most important decision is the decision to act. This is the most essential step. If there are four potential courses, the chances are that you can make any of the four work because the *will* to achieve is nine-tenths the achieving.

> *One man with a dream, at pleasure,*
>   *Shall go forth and conquer a crown;*
> *And three with a new song's measure*
>   *Can trample a kingdom down.*

Candor

Candor, when tempered with a sensitivity to others' feelings, is a refreshing breeze in the sometimes impersonal climate of organization life. How often do men reach out for a job they have spent a lifetime preparing for only to have it denied them by some annoying behavior of which they were never aware. If along the way someone had had the courage to tell it as it was, they could have corrected the undesirable habit that blocked their way.

Some men lack the courage to "lay it on" to others. Other men see their associates' weakness as a personal advantage to them. It eliminates a potential competitor. Still others are so engrossed in their own pursuits as to be insensitive to other people's conditions. These are

"He who rebukes a man will afterward find more favor than he who flatters with his tongue."
Ancient Proverb

not the true leaders of men. Your success as a manager is built upon the success of others. In the words of the ancient proverb, "He who rebukes a man will afterward find more favor than he who flatters with his tongue."

Candor is no license for picking another person to pieces, nor is it an excuse for rudeness. It must have a constructive purpose. As one executive expressed it, "Say it if you think it, but don't say it just because you think you should."

You must establish your credibility if you would have others accept your frankness with an open mind. Old and close friends can say things to each other that would be insulting if they came from a stranger. Your aim should be to suggest without judgment and to criticize without condemnation.

. . . suggest without judgment and . . . criticize without condemnation.

Separate the person from the act you are criticizing! The other person should not be made to feel that he has lost your respect because of an error in action. If you still have his respect—and if he has his own self-respect—he will be receptive to doing something about the offending actions. A smile does amazing things in easing the tensions and reducing the agony of frankness.

After criticism, assure the person that his actions have not compromised your personal relationships with him. One way of doing this is to seek the person out in a location different from the one in which the previous discussion was held—his work place, the company lunch room, etc.—and conversing with him on some unrelated topic.

Candor has another important dimension. The manager who is open and above board and who tells it "straight out" will gain a sense of loyalty in his associates that he can earn in no other way. When people come to know they will get straight answers, they much more readily accept them. People are more comfortable *knowing* the worst than they are in *imagining* just how bad things are. "Present fears are always less than horrible imaginings."—Hamlet

Decisiveness

The effective manager is capable of making the key decisions that keep things moving. While it is often difficult to make a decision, it is even more difficult to leave the decision alone once you have made it. Some managers approach decision-making in the fashion of the child at the penny candy counter: "Let me have one of those, two of those, and one of those; no, instead of two of those, let me have one of these and one of these, then let me . . . ."

To the indecisive manager, a decision carries no commitment; it is merely a way of getting an unpleasant task behind him. Speaking of such a manager, a frustrated employee observed, "Well, it doesn't really matter what he decides; if we just complain loudly enough, he'll change it."

Decisiveness means making decisions that stick. An equivocal decision that changes with the winds of chance is no decision at all. Vacillating direction disrupts the enterprise and destroys confidence in the continuity of affairs. A decision arrived at through sound reasoning then consistently implemented sets a steady course. Decisions that waver undermine the stability of the enterprise.

It is also important, however, that you separate decisiveness from foolhardiness. If your decisions are right, they should stand. When they prove to be wrong, take your losses and change direction.

In gathering facts, you can take a page from the engineering discipline where design concepts are tested before a design is completed. Until his design has been proved in actual "hardware", the design engineer makes no final decision. You may not always have the time for reflection available to the design engineer, but his practice of test and check and test again is a sound method for whatever time you have.

When you anticipate the type of information you will need for the critical issues of your responsibility, you will arrange to have it on tap when you need it. If you are a production foreman, for instance, you would want to maintain a complete record of production hours per part in order to estimate production for new schedules.

Effective leaders are " often wrong but never in doubt." Leaders inspire others to believe in an idea that may

Effective leaders are often wrong but never in doubt.

have nothing to commend it but the determined conviction of one man. He may often be wrong; but more often than not, dynamic action itself will make it right.

The line between a correct course and a wrong one is very narrow, and the distance between then shifts with the tides of time. What is right today may be wrong tomorrow, and what is wrong today may be right tomorrow. Your forcefulness and inspiration will do much to determine the success of the course you have set. This is especially true in marketing, for many sales originate in the mind of the salesman. The salesman who is convinced that he will make the sale gets dramatically greater results than the one who doubts his chances.

One of the harshest criticisms that can be leveled at an executive is, "He just can't make a decision." Whatever place President Harry Truman will have in the Presidential Hall of Fame, he will owe largely to his spunky determination and forceful decisions. Friends and enemies alike admired Truman for his forceful and conclusive actions. His famous phrase, "The buck stops here" has become a byword in the lexicon of executive wisdom.

Leaders inspire others to believe in an idea that may have nothing to commend it but the determined conviction of one man.

Judgment

Judgment is the ability to evaluate a set of events and decide what the advantageous response should be. A sound judgment is the one made at a time when conditions are favorable for constructive results. Until the setting is conducive to the response, the decisive act fails its purpose.

When do you know that the time is ripe for a decision? The experienced manager will say, "You can feel it," but this doesn't help much when you have no "feel".

Here are the types of signals that help give you that feel:

First: Are you at a crossroad where a decision must be made to keep people from being idle?

Second: Are there matters of personal safety or employee working conditions involved?

Third: Will action now create a positive response from other people?

Fourth: Do the people (perhaps the "old hands") who best know the conditions and the opportunities believe that it is time to act?

Fifth: Does the organization have the finances, facilities, supplies, and people necessary to handle the proposed course?

Sixth: Is there a precedent from similar circumstances in the past?

Seventh: Do standard company policies or practices dictate a particular course?

In forming a judgment, lay your heart void of fore-taken opinions.

People's judgments improve in proportion to their ability to remove themselves from the personal consequences of those judgments. Wellington said, "I mistrust the judgment of every man in a case in which his own wishes are concerned."

If you have no pre-conceived ideas, your chances of making the correct judgment are improved; when you have such pre-conceived ideas, the prophets remind us, "In forming a judgment, lay your heart void of fore-taken opinions."

All too often we shape our evidence to prove our opinions. Many years ago a large company decided to expand its capacity by building a new plant. Some top corporate directors decided where they wanted it to be. They then asked their commercial research department to determine the most efficient location for serving present and future markets—hoping that the studies would prove the correctness of the selected location. Several different studies were made, and each time the answer dictated a location other than the one that had been decided upon. Finally, an exasperated executive said, "Well, just change your numbers until you show the results we want." The plant was actually built in the location preferred by the corporate executives, and for many years it operated with poor results.

The application of judgment demands two things: *First,* a clear perception of relative values. *Second,* a reasonable ordering of priorities. In the course of your managerial life you will encounter individuals who vehemently contend for some trivial matter. If you make an issue of an irrelevant point merely to prove someone wrong, you only strengthen that person's willful opposition. If such a person insists on being wrong on a peripheral issue, it is time wasted to argue the point. Let him be wrong.

According to an ancient Persian prophet, "Fortune is for all; judgment is theirs who have won it by themselves." Life is all too often an endless chain of "dreary labor and lonely thought." Yet it is in the caldron of our most personal experiences that we hammer out the rationale of our own judgments. Here are the types of questions you should ask yourself about issues on which you must enter a judgment:

1. What actions will best serve the long-term well-being of the enterprise?
2. Are the potential rewards of this course significantly greater than those of other courses; if not, are there other reasons that justify this course?
3. Does the enterprise have the capability of meeting the demands that this course will place upon it?
4. Is my judgment compatible with the course of others with whom action must be coordinated?
5. Is my judgment consistent with my past actions or with the judgments of others who have gone before me; if not, is there adequate evidence to support a departure from past practice?
6. Will others understand and support my decision? If there is any doubt about this, am I able to explain and justify my action?

"Fortune is for all; judgment is theirs who have won it by themselves."

Persian Prophet

Responsibility

To be responsible simply means to assume the consequences of one's decisions and judgments. The responsible person does not shirk the burden of taking a position. He does not back away from the thought of "sticking his neck out". He willingly—even eagerly—assumes the full credit or blame for his actions. He has learned to accept the outcome of his decisions.

The responsible person is the mature person. Joshua Liebman expressed it this way, "[The mature person has] . . . completed the evolution from parasite to patron, from taking child and fighting adolescent, to giving adult."

As you look back upon your own work experience, you can probably identify the stages of your own growth. First, you were completely dependent upon others. Then you struggled to be free. Finally, you gained a capacity to give of yourself to other people. If you were lucky, you were not placed in managerial responsibility until you attained this third level. If you were thrust into it before you reached the third stage, you either matured very rapidly on the job, or you experienced some failure. The chances are that even now you still have some growing to do. Most of us do.

The responsible manager stands with his associates on the outcome of their common effort. A cynic once described the clever manager as one who assumes all credit and assigns all blame. The true leader accepts the full results of his actions whether they be credit or blame—the so-called "clever" manager does not usually survive.

The responsible person is as good as his word. If he says he will do something, you can count on it. We have all known those people who, when they say it will rain

> "[The mature person has] . . . completed the evolution from parasite to patron, from taking child and fighting adolescent, to giving adult."
>
> Joshua Liebman

tomorrow, cause us to reach for our umbrellas. To develop this type of reliability—and it is an incalculable asset for you as a manager—make sure you can deliver on your commitments. Before you agree to a course of action or commit yourself, know what will be expected of you. Just as in the law, the plea of ignorance is no excuse for your failure to do what other people have come to expect of you.

If after you are committed to a particular course, a change in conditions dictates that you change course, you should explain the changed circumstances to those affected—*and get their agreement to the change.* If your "word is as good as your bond", you do not need the temporary gain of a "sharp" deal. A contemporary philosopher expressed it this way: "Much . . . bitterness is spared to him who thinks naturally upon what he owes to others, rather than what he ought to expect from them."

If you are responsible, you are accountable. Nothing will tone up a man's honesty quite like the realization that he is accountable for his actions. If you can't believe in yourself enough to take the consequences of your actions, what else can you believe in?

The scope and breadth of your commitment often stretches beyond your immediate view. Someone has said, "Responsibility's like a string we can only see the middle of. Both ends are out of sight." When you assume the obligation of leadership, your decisions are like the stone dropped on the calm waters of a pool—the ripples move in concentric circles into bays and coves you never see. Your actions as a manager will always have repercussions beyond your immediate ken.

John D. Rockefeller Jr. from his eminent position in the affairs of industrial enterprise observed, "I believe

. . . the plea of ignorance is no excuse for your failure to do what other people have come to expect of you.

that every right implies a responsibility; every opportunity, an obligation; and every possession, a duty." Every manager, whether his position be humble or mighty, faces the challenge of responsibility, obligation, and duty.

As you face the demands of your managerial responsibility, your actions cannot be measured solely by their value to you. You are affecting the lives and fortunes of people you will never know or see—employees and their families, people outside the enterprise who deal with it, and the general public in your community. These are sobering implications, and they are present with us in every one of our managerial decisions.

The moment you become a "boss" you expand your responsibility by the sum of the people whose work you direct. You become accountable to every member in your organization. In law, the accountability of the principal for the acts of his agent is very elaborately described. As a manager, you are a principal with full accountability for the acts of your people. You may not have the legal liability of the principal for his agent, but you are just as accountable for the actions of others. You are judged by what others do even more than by what you do yourself. Since you will get the credit, you are also entitled to the blame.

Responsibility walks hand in hand with capacity and power. The broader the position, the greater the responsibility. In Nietzche's words, "Life always gets harder toward the summit—the cold increases, responsibility increases."

If you think things are tough now, just wait until you reach the next rung on the ladder. Don't count on it getting any easier. It won't. It might give you a little more perspective and therefore make things a little

"Much . . . bitterness is spared to him who thinks naturally upon what he owes to others, rather than what he ought to expect from them."

Modern Philosopher

easier to understand, but it certainly will get no softer.

Recognizing that you are responsible for the acts of others, you will want to establish a system for keeping yourself informed on their performance. The subject of performance review is a major topic in its own right, but here are some of the major tools for keeping tab on your responsibility:

> **First,** define the job to be performed. This is done in a number of ways: Position Descriptions, Position Specifications, Organizational Charts.
>
> **Second,** prescribe the specific tasks and the schedules within which they should be achieved: performance standards, operating plans, operating objectives.
>
> **Third,** develop performance records that show operating results: schedule performance, costs, quality.
>
> **Fourth,** appraise results against standards and objectives and take any necessary corrective action either in changing goals or reinforcing performance.

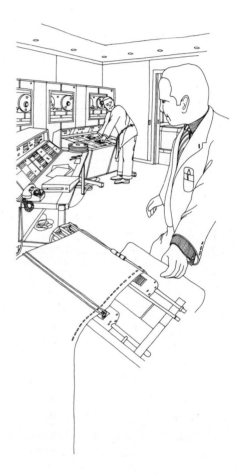

Responsibility is as essential in management as is timing on the trapeze bar. Both are the by-product of disciplined practice. Just as the trapeze artist's split-second timing results from hours of coordinated practice, so responsibility results from the exercise of making decisions and accepting the consequences of those decisions.

Command

By command we mean that state of being in which a person is in control of himself. People unusually gifted with this capacity are characterized as having *Presence*. The world, it is said, makes way for the man who knows where he is going. Such a person knows his capabilities, and he radiates an air of confidence born of knowing what he can do. Rabelais said, "How shall I be able to rule over others and have not full power and command of myself."

The effective manager acknowledges his dependency on other people. You do not have to be right every time. When you acknowledge your errors and amend your mistakes, you strengthen your relationships with others. By admitting yourself to the human family of the imperfect, you show that you are in control of the situation.

From your position as the "boss", you can compel others to accept your authority. The authoritarian approach, however, sacrifices the willing support so essential to sustained performance. If people perform only because of the authority of their leaders, the enterprise is like a motor vehicle running with its brakes on. Shakespeare's MacBeth saw the folly of sheer power:

> *Those he commands move only in command,*
> *Nothing in love. Now does he feel his title*
> *Hang loose about him, like a giant's robe*
> *Upon a dwarfish thief.*

It has been said that power corrupts, and absolute power corrupts absolutely. The heady sense of power that comes to a man in a position to control other men's lives is exhilarating, but all too often it leads to a blind use of that power and to a false sense of omnipotence.

In Plato's ideal state, *The Republic,* the leaders are philosophers: men whose seasoned experience give them the wisdom and understanding to view their actions and the actions of others in a broad perspective.

Plato's wisdom is abundantly clear to those who watch the brilliant but judgment-lacking leader. The gift of command is not an automatic consequence of chronological age, for many men never seem to acquire it. Indeed, young people often display more of it than their elders. In general, however, command is a product of the confidence compounded from varieties of experience.

"He is a fool who cannot be angry, but he is a wise man who will not."

English Proverb

A successful executive explained his own development in these words: "I was considered for this Vice-President job fifteen years ago when I was thirty-two years old. Fortunately for me, it didn't come to me then, for it would have been a terrible struggle. Now I can handle it with relative ease—and no tension." The opportunity for leadership comes to men of all ages. The great challenge is to know when you have acquired the practical and philosophical resources to lead other men.

One of man's most fascinating traits is his pure "cussedness", as Mark Twain would have said it. A social creature he is, but a supine creature he is not. He will not willingly subjugate himself to the autocratic dominance of a fellow human. When we finally learn that "a man convinced against his will is of the same opinion still," we realize the folly of trying to mold other people into our ways. We rely instead upon the power of self-motivation. Assuming that we have selected able people, when we get them involved in the decisions that affect their individual jobs, we direct their normal drives into productive channels.

An old English proverb says, "He is a fool who cannot be angry, but he is a wise man who will not." Great leaders are always slow to anger; and while they can be angry, they know that decisions made in anger are doomed to failure. An intemperate tirade may yield a grudging action, but it does not motivate. The victim of a dressing down may do what he is ordered to do, but he will hardly do it with any enthusiasm.

The next time you feel the need to vent your spleen, ask yourself how you would react if you were the recipient. The one in full command of himself does not beat around the bush, but he does not dismember his victim.

Only when a man has learned to take directions can he be fully effective in giving them. When you know what it is like to be on the receiving end, you can know what to expect from that end. As a manager, one of your greatest challenges is to predict the response of those to whom you are privileged to give direction. If you have put in your time "toiling in the vineyards", you will know what to expect. You will not always be able to predict others' responses, but you will certainly have fewer surprises.

When you are sensitive to your own reactions and aware of the reactions of others, you are gaining command. When you have mastered yourself and when you anticipate the expectations and motivations of others, you will have attained command.

30

Skills

The previous discussion dealt with modes of managerial behavior and attitudes. The following pages are concerned with specific techniques and methods by which managers carry out their varied responsibilities.

Organization

One of your first acts as a manager should be to establish the range of your responsibility—to find out what is expected of you and to determine the scope of your authority. Once you have your own charter clearly established, you will then be able to pass on to your associates a definition of their responsibility and authority. In this way, your associates can relate their own expectations to the expectations of the enterprise. When you thus establish a basic plan of the game, and—even more important—when you play the game according to that plan, you eliminate nine tenths of the lethargy that plagues poorly organized groups.

People differ greatly in their need for structured patterns of behavior. Some people require a great deal of structure and others need very little. It appears, however, that everyone requires some degree of organization.

Even the poet, the most free and unstructured of the literary artists, deals in *patterns*. While he may achieve an understanding of those patterns in a relatively free manner and while he may express them in a similarly free manner, he tries to get us to comprehend some *pattern* as he sees it. He *organizes* his thoughts to convey a meaning to us.

Human organizations fulfill their purposes through the performance of specific tasks. Those tasks range

32

from the routine to the creative. Man's constant struggle
to rise above the level of brute animal has enabled him
to assign many of the more dreary duties to the machine.
In any human enterprise, however, there are many routine duties left for man to perform.

The purpose of organizing work is to assure that it
will be performed in the most effective manner and thus
with the least burden. By organizing we minimize the
demand on our time and give ourselves the opportunity
to develop the creative and innovative aspects of our
responsibility. Equally important, as a manager, when
you know that essential tasks are being efficiently performed by others, you can concentrate your time on the
human dynamics of your managerial job.

The specific techniques that you use to organize your
particular activities will vary with the breadth and scope
of your responsibilities, but the following methods are
widely used:

> **First,** a statement of basic responsibility for each
> position. A Position Description for non-supervisory
> positions and a basic Statement of Responsibility
> for supervisory positions. (Since supervision is
> basically the same at whatever level it is found, a
> single statement for managerial positions and an-
> other for supervisory positions will cover most
> requirements.)
>
> **Second,** an organization chart when it is desirable
> to show relationships between positions and de-
> partments.
>
> **Third,** objectives to be met: specific performance
> results to be attained and standards of performance
> for specific tasks. Included here could be standard
> cost data, production goals, and profit ratios.

One school of thought deliberate-ly pits one person against another on the theory that "natural" competitive drive is wholesome. The consequences of such tactics are more divisive than constructive.

Fourth, policies—the basic ground rules—governing the conduct of affairs in the organization.

Fifth, procedures showing the sequential steps by which tasks are performed.

Sixth, for any activities in which the sequences or relationships between various activities are particularly intricate, work flow charts help in coordinating the various activities.

Seventh, standard practices such as standard production operations for established product lines.

Eighth, operating plans and schedules for overall operations or for specific departmental activities. Included here would be such elements as market forecasts, new product development schedules, cash flow forecasts, or production department schedules.

Ninth, standard instructions describing the steps to be followed in performing a particular task or in processing the company's standard documents.

Tenth, schedule of compensation scales and individual compensation rates.

Eleventh, schedule of performance data to keep you informed of results in the various areas of your responsibility. This could include data on such items as product costs, production schedule performance, inventory cost ratios, financial indexes of operating performance, and accident rates.

Motivation

Your first step in motivating people is to find the right people for the right job. There are two basic considerations here: *First,* identify the talents necessary for performing specific jobs; and *Second,* find the people who possess the required talents.

Until you have placed people in jobs for which they are qualified, you have little hope of motivating anybody. When people are challenged by their jobs, they will respond by reaching beyond their immediate performance requirements. Without a continuing challenge and a goal that he can't quite reach, man soon loses the zest for his job.

Notice what happens when you stimulate a person to something beyond his immediate grasp—not too far beyond, but enough that he must stretch for it. That's a good rule for your own job—give yourself a goal that you haven't attained before.

As you staff the various positions in your organization, keep a clear path for each person. If too many able people are aiming for the same goal, a collision is inevitable. One school of thought deliberately pits one person against another on the theory that "natural" competitive drive is wholesome. The consequences of such tactics are more divisive than constructive. When five men are being groomed for the same position, it is inevitable that four will be demoralized and their effectiveness diminished. In most situations, such collision courses are avoidable.

The manager's responsibility can be likened to that of the plant engineer charged with maintaining plant equipment. If he does his job properly, there are no breakdowns and no production stoppages. He keeps the machinery humming and the facilities in top condition. Your task as a manager is to keep the human machinery in peak condition. This requires your attention to human needs just as the plant engineer devotes his attention to the plant equipment.

Employee work performance is your primary concern, but you must be sensitive to outside pressures that infringe upon an employee's time or distract him from his job. While you have no right to inject yourself into an employee's personal life, you should recognize that unusual conditions in his life will affect his performance.

When you strive to motivate people to the creative use of their talents, you will discover surprising and fascinating opportunities—opportunities that will have escaped even those people themselves. The emotional and mental security created by personalized attention fosters a dedication to the job that all the pay increases in the world cannot buy.

. . . people will perform what is expected of them: if the goal is high, their performance will be high; if the goal is low, performance will be low.

Goal Setting

Charles Mangel, Senior Editor of *Look* magazine, takes the American people to task for the quality of American life,

> *"We are a slipshod people. We tend to do nothing unless a crisis is at hand, and then we seek simplistic, temporary measures . . . . Civilization is not a matter of museums and global communications. It derives from a quality of mind and of concern. And by that definition, we, of course, are not a civilized nation at all, rather a self-centered, stupid one. And the soothing words of all our politicians, all our churchmen, all our 'important' people matter not. We are incompetent."*

If Mr. Mangel is correct, we have been satisfied with unworthy goals. It is difficult to accept this appraisal of America at face value, and Mr. Mangel probably had tongue in cheek as he said it. It is true, nonetheless, that in spite of our astounding technological achievements, we are often content to settle for mediocrity.

The pursuit of a higher goal has been at the root of American life, and there are innumerable examples of outstanding achievement in all walks of life. While we may be enticed to accept less, why should we settle for less than the best when with very little extra effort we can usually have it? Ray Bradbury, the dean of science-fiction writers, admonishes the aspiring young writer, "Do your own thing, but whatever you do, do it the best way you know how—*excellence is the key to success* in this business."

Quality is usually equated with excellence, but *quality* is a relative term whereas *excellence* is absolute. There are ranges of quality—grade 1, grade 2, grade 3, etc.—but excellence applies to each grade. If you are in the automobile business, for example, a $4,000.00 car may represent grade 3 and a $12,000.00 car may represent grade 1. Each one of these, however, could be excellent for its particular niche in the quality structure. Excellence means doing whatever you do in the best way that current knowledge permits. In the $4,000.00 automobile it is just as important that the brakes work well or that the body be free of rattles as it is in the $12,000.00 car. Such results require a commitment to excellence.

Experience teaches us that people will perform what is expected of them: if the goal is high, their performance will be high; if the goal is low, performance will be low.

The formula for excellence in human enterprise consists of two basic elements: *Quality and Service*. If the enterprise serves a lasting human need, if it delivers its product/service at a time and in a form desired by its

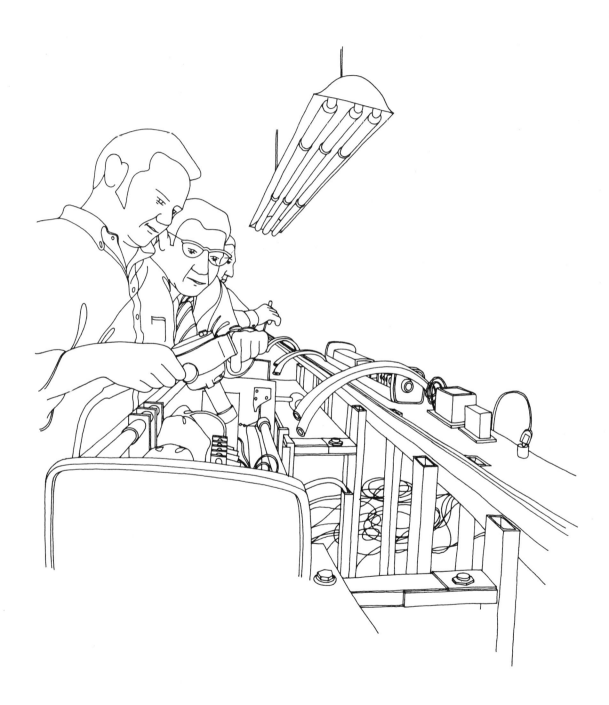

customers, and if the quality of that product/service remains at a level consistent with the customer's expectations, the acceptance of the product is assured. It is the manager's responsibility to establish and maintain these goals at the highest level the enterprise is capable of attaining.

Your goal or the goal of your enterprise may be for a high level of quality or a low. There are great ranges in individual requirements, and there are plenty of customers for whatever quality level you decide to offer. Some people will demand only the highest quality, others will want less, and still others will want only the barest minimum. The important thing is that quality, at whatever level it is established, be *consistent* and that the service be *compatible* with the established level. At whatever quality you choose, if you perform *excellently,* you will be assured of consistent quality.

Once your goals are set, your next step is to establish realistic operating objectives. Objectives may entail a considerable variety of matters, but they usually evolve around three elements: *costs, schedules,* and *quality.* For each of these elements, you could establish desired levels or ratios. You can then use these levels and ratios to measure accomplishments.

1. **Cost:** The dollars required to perform the task—manhours, materials, and services.
2. **Schedule:** The time within which the task is to be completed.
3. **Quality:** The quality level to be met.

Discipline

Discipline has two meanings: *First,* the imposition of sanctions for infraction of a rule or for improper execution of an assignment; *Second,* the degree to which members control themselves in carrying out their tasks (self-discipline). The former is a type of punishment; the latter reflects the degree of dedication with which people pursue their tasks. If a manager must discipline (punish) someone, he has already lost most of his effectiveness in motivating that person. If the purpose of discipline is to correct behavior, punishment defeats its purpose because punishment merely suppresses behavior—it does not redirect it.

Your aim as a manager should be to seek constructive ways of encouraging people to a self-disciplined exercise of their responsibilities. The word *discipline* derives from the Latin word for *learning.* When you "discipline" others, your aim should be to see that they learn to establish their own rules.

Punishment is effective only when imposed by a person upon himself in a resolve to overcome a past error. Most people know when they have "goofed". If encouraged to do so, they will correct their own errors. The popular "chewing out" strengthens the person's determination to avoid the boss's ire by concealing errors rather than correcting them.

A disciplined work force is not a regimented force where members fall into lock-step upon the command of their leader. While you may occasionally wish you could get people working with such mechanical precision, the most productive environment is the one where each person controls (disciplines) himself in pursuing the goals of the enterprise.

The popular "chewing out" strengthens the person's determination to avoid the boss's ire by concealing errors rather than correcting them.

Your aim should be to foster a sense of self-interest and self-growth through self-discipline. There are numerous ways to stimulate this attitude:

First, Restrain your impulse to tell a person how to do his job—especially when you once had the same job.

Second, In developing specific operating objectives, consult with affected persons and get them involved in setting the objectives. In this way, they will feel committed to the goals.

Third, When things go wrong, ask the person involved what he thinks went wrong and how he believes he can correct it *before* you give your version. If your analysis and conclusions are different from his, be prepared to explain why.

Fourth, When a reprimand is necessary, do it in a place apart from the person's immediate area of work and away from the hearing of others. Above all, avoid putting it in writing.

Fifth, Keep your eye on what's going on. When you see something that will interfere with getting a job done, tell someone about it.

Sixth, Don't pussyfoot around an issue. When you observe a condition that needs correcting, speak out.

Seventh, When someone asks you for an answer to his problem, help him find his own answer. You are not going to be there all the time, and he needs to establish his own method of dealing with problems as they arise.

Eighth, If someone brings you a complaint about another person, get the two parties together to work out an amicable settlement. Avoid taking sides.

Communication means receptive listening and response—even if the response is only to say "no".

Communication

Communication is the vital artery that nourishes every part of the organization body.

Where you find a highly productive organization with high morale, you will inevitably find that communications flow easily through all segments of the enterprise. People arc aware of what is going on around them, and they know what is expected of them. They feel a part of the organization, and they easily relate their interests to it.

Your written and verbal skills are important, but equally important is your willingness to let others express themselves. Listening is every bit as important as speaking.

The effective communicator explains the reasons behind his message. If the reasons are not understood, he encourages people to ask. As one manager expressed it, "If you can't take it on faith, ask." The reason for an action is often more illuminating than is the action itself; so it is essential that people know what is behind the action.

There will be times when you will want to use communication as a counter-action. Try as you may to keep everyone informed, you will never stop the rumor mill. There will always be someone willing to start a rumor that flashes through the company like a bolt of lightning. Someone has an "inside" story or a "scoop" that tickles everyone's fancy—the big boss is getting the boot, they're closing down the Gumbille plant, or whatever.

Your greatest challenge in combatting the rumor mill is to learn about it. Once you know the rumor—and your secretary is probably your most reliable informant—you must decide whether to set the record straight or to ignore it. When the item is relatively trivial, it is probably best to ignore it; to acknowledge it only gives it credence. When the issue is more substantive, some recognition of it is usually called for.

Over-explanation can be just as damaging as under-explanation. Limit your explanation to the requirements of each situation. Let it go at that. The salesman knows well the art of closing when the sale is made. Many a sale has been lost by the inexperienced salesman who keeps talking after the customer has decided to buy. So it is with the manager; when your communication has met its objective—when the point has been accepted—drop it. Here are some clues that tell you when you've scored your point in verbal communication. Concurrence with written communication will show itself in a similar way, but it will be less immediate.

1. The listener nods his assent or by facial expression shows that he has found someone who sees things as he does.

2. The listener's questions evolve into statements of agreement with the points you are making.

3. The listener stops asking questions, indicating that he no longer has any reservation about what you are saying.

4. The listener restates your ideas in his own words. Some people must verbalize their view before it becomes real to them.

5. A listener repeats your statement and asserts his agreement with it, and others in the group show their assent to the listener's statement.

6. A person who had earlier expressed a disagreement acknowledges a change in his point of view.

Effective communication implies availability. If you are to make the most of your opportunity, you must be available to the people who have a message for you. Many managers pride themselves on their "open door" availability, declaring they always see the people who wish to see them and that they can always be approached. Availability is more than physical presence. It means receptive listening and response—even if the response is only to say "no".

Credibility is vital. You must not only explain yourself; you must follow through on your commitments. When you make known what you intend to do, you must either do it or give a plausible explanation for any subsequent event that dictates a change in your course.

44

Follow-up is essential. When others are to carry out the action, your follow-up instills confidence that you are aware of what is going on. When you are responsible for the action and when other people are aware that some action is pending, they will want to know how it works out.

The art of timing is important. You must know when to explain and when to withhold; when to speak out and when to remain silent; and when to seek out an explanation and when not to press for one. In the course of human events there are some things better left unsaid. Witness this case of a delicate corporate merger:

A company marketing director was disturbed by what seemed to be a questionable business transaction in a contract negotiated between one of his salesmen and a major distributor. The new contract included an option clause for representation into "extended territories". The customer's general manager had confided in the salesman about his plans to acquire another distributor, but he could not make a public disclosure. The salesman would have been placed in an embarrassing position if forced to explain the details to his boss. When pressed for an explanation of the unusual terms, the salesman asked if he could defer an explanation. Wisely, the marketing director did not press the matter. Had he done so, he could have seriously compromised the salesman's future dealings with the customer. In this case, a silent communication was every bit as significant as a detailed explanation.

Communication is the vital artery that nourishes every part of the organization body.

Direction

Clark Clifford, U.S. Secretary of Defense in the Johnson administration, was characterized as a ". . . highly methodical, analytical man who will be nobody's pigeon." In describing his approach to the job, Mr. Clifford explained how an executive must "mix it up" in the day-to-day affairs of his enterprise. Of his job as Secretary of Defense he said,

> *"The scope of the problems is wider than anyone can imagine until he actually comes in contact with them. I am beginning to perceive the great number of decisions that the Secretary must make himself. He cannot sit back and confine himself to high-level policy pronouncements. He must get into the thick of it."*

One view of the managerial job is that the manager studies the "Big Picture", forms a judgment, and makes his decision. The experienced executive knows this is pure fantasy. You must know the circumstances that give rise to the need for a decision, and the only way you can do this is to get your hands on as many facts, opinions, and ideas as possible. You will often make decisions "off the cuff", but behind these actions is an unconscious search-and-sort through innumerable data stored in your head from past experience.

Search as you will for positive proof of the validity of your course, you will never find it. As someone has said, "Management can be defined as making decisions based on inadequate information." You should be at least as willing to gamble on your managerial judgments as you are to gamble on your life when you get into your automobile. You can control—most of the time—your own car, but you have no control over the other driver. So it is in management: your decisions will be at the mercy

Management can be defined as making decisions based on inadequate information.

of forces you can never see. But you can't let that stop you. The accident reports do not keep you out of your automobile.

Recognizing that you cannot be as familiar with all the areas of your organization as the people who work in those areas, you can employ your communications in such a way as to let these people know you are aware of their capabilities and their knowledge of the job. No one expects you to have all the answers. There is no need to try to convince them that you do. They know better. Even more important, however, they want a chance to tell you what they know. They're usually convinced that no one really cares.

Work direction in the form of a question rather than a command is doubly effective: *First,* it places you in the position of assisting rather than demanding; and *second,* it opens the mind of the recipient as command can never do.

The concept of the manager as a "power" is an outmoded idea in this era of intense specialization and high technology. The notion of domination, while popular in the school of authoritarian leadership, is a poor substitute for motivation. A leading psychologist observed, "In the future, doing things to people, along with gaining control over people, may well become as unfashionable as it is fruitless."

The only meaningful control is that which each person exercises over himself. For anyone, whether manager, parent, or army general, to assume he can get maximum productivity by the exercise of power alone is indulging in the grossest form of self-delusion. You should aim to make it possible for people to get a little of their own egos into their jobs. Charles H. Steinway, the great piano maker, once said, "I cannot commend to a business house any artificial plan for making men producers .... You must lead them through self-interest."

To say that as a manager you must "walk softly" is not to say that you can abdicate your responsibility. It is the *way* you use your responsibility that's important. You will always get the best results when you encourage self-motivation. Since you can never be there all the time, your best course is to support people in the use of their own initiative.

One of the most important events in a company's affairs is the arrival of a new employee. You have a special responsibility for introducing the employee to his new "home", not only to assure that he is properly oriented but to introduce him to the company's way of doing things. As a part of his instruction on the group's method and business practices, you ought to make it clear that, in the beginning, he should consult you rather than to go to other employees for interpretations or explanations of the company's methods.

The surest way of emasculating a business system is to let the new employee get his indoctrination from an "old timer". How many times have you heard a new employee say,

"Well, I didn't know how you did it here; so I asked John, and he told me."

John often doesn't know, but he tries to be helpful and says what he thinks is best. If he is a "curbstone lawyer", he may say,

"Well, the book says you should do it this way; but that's not the way we actually do it."

If there is something wrong with the "book", the manager should be the first to know; but until the prescribed

"In the future, doing things to people, along with gaining control over people, may well become as unfashionable as it is fruitless."
A Leading Psychologist

method is changed, the job should be done the way the instructions say it.

The new employee should not, of course, be restricted from communicating with other employees. Until he is completely familiar with the requirements of his new job, however, you should be the one to instruct him on company practices and policies.

Timing is most important. Shakespeare summed this up in those famous lines from Julius Caesar:

> There is a tide in the affairs of men,
>   Which, taken at the flood, leads on to fortune;
> Omitted, all the voyage of their life
>   Is bound in shallows and in miseries . . . .
> We must take the current when it serves,
>   Or lose our ventures.

When you keep yourself alert to what other people are doing and thinking, you know when someone is bewildered or confused, when work is bottlenecked, when quality rejections are high, and when a customer is planning a plant expansion. The surest way to keep abreast of what is going on is to circulate, to keep in touch with people in their work places.

The new manager will never make it as a manager until he learns to let others make their own mistakes.

Delegation

The importance of delegation is evidenced by the emphasis given to it in all serious discussion of management. Delegation in its basic elements simply means that a manager divides up the total scope of things his organization has to do, assumes certain of these tasks himself, and assigns the remaining ones to other people. This process seems simple enough, but effective delegation necessitates a delicate balance between too little and too much. There are two pitfalls to avoid: over-delegation or abdication; and under-delegation or chaos.

The abdicating manager assigns tasks to "get them out of his hair". In effect, he says he does not want to be bothered with the task, and he hopes he won't hear about it again. All too often, the abdicator is looking for someone on whom to pin the blame if things do not turn out well. He is always willing, of course, to accept the credit for anything that does turn out well.

The second form of unskilled delegation—under-delegation—is the most common pitfall for the new manager. He does not yet realize that he must rely on other people to do things that he had previously done himself. When he is forced to give a task to someone else, he inwardly clings to the belief that he could do it better himself—and he is usually right. He watches and second-guesses the assignee and finally ends up doing the job himself. He'll never make it as a manager until he learns to let others make their own mistakes.

The inevitable plea of the under-delegator is, "If you want something done right, you have to do it yourself." Such a person has not yet recognized that he can never do it all himself and that he must learn to keep "hands off".

You must ultimately reconcile yourself to the fact that your success lies in the hands of other people even more than in your own.

Effective delegation combines self-restraint and tactics. You must ultimately reconcile yourself to the fact that your success lies in the hands of other people even more than in your own. Until you learn to trust the potential soundness of others' judgments, there will be no effective delegation. You may occasionally be disappointed, even humiliated, by another's poor performance. The solution is to improve your techniques of directing and coaching, not to take over the task yourself.

The following steps will help to insure effective delegation:

1. Identify the activity to be performed and explain whether it is a permanent and continuing assignment or a one-time task.

2. Describe the results expected and the estimated time within which they are to be achieved.

3. Decide on the person or group to whom the activity is to be assigned; then communicate the nature

of the activity, the results to be expected, and the time within which the activity is to be completed.

4. Ascertain that the activity has been executed and that the results have been attained.

5. Evaluate the results to determine the effectiveness of the execution and the correctness of the original assignment.

Challenge

A seasoned chief executive once said that he lost interest in job candidates who were "looking for a challenge".

"Challenge", he contended, "is with us everyday in every act we perform—from getting to work in the morning over a crowded highway to closing a large order with a new account—and a person does not have to look for a job with challenge; every job is full of challenges."

You know better than anyone else the challenges in your organization. It is in your hands to dramatize those challenges.

To be challenged means to be involved in the vital affairs of the enterprise. This, in turn, means to be aware of one's own impact on those affairs. Nothing is so demoralizing as to feel that one's efforts are of little consequence. It is your role to help each person realize the value of his job. You can do this in two ways:

> **First,** keep your people informed about the activities and goals of the enterprise so they will feel a part of it. Not everyone, of course, will display a high degree of enthusiasm for his work. Your aim should be to get your people involved in and committed to the enterprise. Martin Luther King, speaking of neglected people everywhere, eloquently expressed

"No society can suffer any greater tragedy than to cause its members to feel that they have no stake in their society."
Martin Luther King

the vital necessity of involvement, "No society can suffer any greater tragedy than to cause its members to feel that they have no stake in their society."

Second, make each person realize that he is important to the welfare of the enterprise. Help everyone (and no glossy public relations promotion campaign can ever do the job) to see that the work he performs is important and that if he were absent, his contribution would be missed. When each member comes to realize that his associates depend on him to get their own work done, he will recognize that when he fails to do his job, he is letting his associates down. (If you can't say in good conscience that each person is really essential to the group's efforts, you have too many people on the payroll.)

. . . people are inspired by example, not rhetoric.

The plant manager of a large company cogently described the feeling of futility that comes over a person when he realizes his work is of small significance to his organization:

> "I have been with this company for twenty-five years and am now in a position where I regularly make million dollar decisions. But the frustrating part about it is that I can make the company a million or lose them a million, and no one ever knows the difference. I would rather take the rap for a mistake once in awhile. Then I would at least know someone is aware that I'm around."

The best challenge is the challenge of which you yourself are an example. "Never has a man who was bent himself been able to make others straight." If you expect your associates to be straightforward with you, you must be straightforward with them. If you expect them to be dedicated to their jobs, they will take their example from you. It is fruitless to try to beg off with, "Do as I say, not as I do." This just doesn't stand up; people are inspired by example, not rhetoric.

When we influence another person to find a better way, we challenge him. If we wish to inspire a person to move from where he is to where he wants to be, we must first be sure we know where he is—and that he knows it too. This requires that we give our attention to the condition in which other people find themselves.

Persuasion

Heeding the advice that "Compulsion is contrary to nature", the skilled manager recognizes that people do not function effectively under coercion. Even beyond the considerations of human decency, the institution of human slavery inevitably fails because of its gross inefficiency. So it is with the lesser forms of tyranny. The person living in mortal fear of his job is hobbled in his pursuit of that job. While hunger does breed a certain degree of effort, the threat of deprivation will not sustain a high level of productivity. Optimum performance requires a positive commitment. The manager cannot demand that commitment. He elicits it by example and opportunity.

The manager who thinks that being the "boss" will ensure the execution of his directions is in for a rude awakening. As expressed by the title of a best-selling book, he must Persuade or Perish. He must see to it

Compulsion is contrary to nature.

that people are sold on the purposes of the enterprise and on the importance of their roles in it. A "slick" sales pitch is fruitless. The only effective persuasion is a straightforward explanation that separates fancy from fact and that tells it like it is.

If a person cannot accept a situation as it actually is, telling it for what it is not compounds the problem by adding a falsehood to an already unpalatable situation. Most of us recognize that outright deception serves no purpose, but we often create an air of deception by not going far enough in our explanations. Even though a particular task may be onerous, by explaining its purpose you remove all the anxiety and much of the burden. In fact, if you approach the matter imaginatively, the arduous task can be the most stimulating one.

Methods of explanation vary greatly with individual personalities and with varying situations; but by far the more effective technique is a simple, logical, and straightforward exposition of essential conditions and circumstances. While special situations may call for different courses, the most effective approach is to explain the background and describe the results desired. When the end result is understood, the method for attaining that result can be seen in much clearer perspective.

A common failing in selling ideas is the tendency to describe the proposed result before the listener even knows why any result is desirable. By stating your conclusion before you explain the problem, you encourage the listener to form his opinion before he understands the reasons for your conclusion.

. . . life cannot exist without reciprocal concessions.

The inexperienced salesman tends to start his sales pitch in the middle of his story, forgetting that while he knows what goes before, his listener probably hasn't heard that part of the story. The manager, just as the salesman, must learn to start at the beginning of his story and take the listener through to the end, step by step.

In the press of your everyday responsibilities you cannot spend all your time in salesmanship, but no one expects you to. If you have established your credibility and if you regularly communicate with your associates, elaborate explanations will not be necessary.

Persuasion must allow for compromise and the give-and-take of various points of view. Some people operate as though they believe, as Emerson expressed it, that

"Compromise is never anything but an ignoble truce between the duty of a man and the terror of a coward."

The truth is that life cannot exist without reciprocal concessions. The critical consideration is to determine those issues that are absolutely essential and those that are merely desirable. In this way, then, you know where you can give ground and where you cannot.

On major issues it is cowardice to abandon your position; on minor ones it is senseless not to. The manager who casually abandons his position at the slightest resistance will not long remain a leader. Neither will the person who refuses to listen when someone finds a flaw in his decision. The wise person accedes to others' ideas when those ideas enhance the soundness of his course. At the same time, he will be firm in quashing ideas that could weaken it. Prudent compromise is a tool of persuasion; expediency hinders persuasion by undermining confidence.

On major issues it is cowardice to abandon your position; on minor ones it is senseless not to.

Your ability to persuade others to your view depends upon the atmosphere you have created. If the environment is one of harmony, ideas will fall on receptive ears. When others know they can rely on your veracity and on the accuracy of what you say, they are ready to believe you.

Consensus

It is difficult to visualize how any group of people could function for long without a broad agreement on purpose and direction. When one person is employed by another, he agrees to render labor in exchange for certain compensation; but an employment relationship entails much more than the exchange of labor for money. As a manager, it is your responsibility to broaden the base of the employment relationship by giving the employee's job a purpose that means something to him.

In certain vital company programs—as in the introduction of a new product line—a broad consensus is essential. This same type of consensus is important in departmental matters when department-wide activities are involved.

Consensus does not mean unanimity. Unanimity means that everyone reach the same *opinion* on the issue. Consensus requires only that everyone agrees some action is necessary and that those who disagree with the majority will subordinate their preferences and support the majority.

Where consensus management is practiced, it is not uncommon to hear, "Well, I don't understand why we want to do it that way; but if Carl thinks we should do it, I'll go along with it." In every group there are persons whose views carry more weight than do those of others. The properly motivated group will be willing to give extra consideration to the judgments of such persons. In a group governed by consensus there will be various positions: some will believe a particular action is right; others will be willing to support the judgments of people who better understand the situation; and still others who disagree on the selected course will accede to the action in order not to hold the group back.

When the consensus approach is called for, the minority unites with the rest of the group to achieve action. Disagreements are settled with the least distress to the least number, and the enterprise moves forward in unity. Such a course represents a more rational and practical solution of basic issues than is the case when a majority forces its will upon the group.

Complete unity is not likely to happen. However, on issues of major importance to the enterprise, there are distinct advantages to the consensus process:

Prudent compromise is a tool of persuasion; expediency hinders persuasion by undermining confidence.

1. While minority members may still have lingering reservations, they will not "lobby" against the final decision. They will let the group go forward without putting obstacles in the way.

2. Individual members, in order to avoid obstructing the group's progress, will not oppose the group unless they have very serious objections. They will tend to be more conscientious and thorough in their appraisal of a proposed action, for their views will be very intensely scrutinized by the group.

3. The group will avoid suppressing any member in the statement of his position.

4. Discussion becomes free and candid. From a mutual respect borne of a common stake in the enterprise, open disagreements and intensive inquiry of others' views will be commonplace. In such deliberations personal relationships reflect mutual respect.

5. Out of recognition that the group is seeking an answer satisfactory to all—not a victory for one or repression of another—defensiveness and anxiety fade. The eventual judgment emerges as a victory for all.

Conclusion

The attributes and skills discussed in this book describe the ideal manager. They are the universal characteristics of leadership. It would be unrealistic to expect one person to attain all these skills or develop all these attributes. Indeed, some traits may even be incompatible with others. You should seek a balance, selecting those practices that best suit your particular temperament and style.

To some extent it can be said, as it can of all occupations, that great managers are born, not made. But, given the desire and the motivation, the trained and disciplined person will always outclass a gifted individual content to rest on his laurels.

While we have yet much to learn about identifying the meaning of basic personality traits, some characteristics of temperament and disposition are undoubtedly necessary to management. To the extent that the reader can relate his personality to the blueprint described here, he will have a foundation for building the attributes and skills of management.

Whatever your personality, these are the challenges you face. If they fit you, your adventure can be both fascinating and noble.

When you assume the obligation of leadership, your decisions are like the stone dropped on the calm waters of a pool—the ripples move in concentric circles into bays and coves you never see.

The Creative Management Center

The purpose of the Creative Management Center is to expand the capabilities of managers through the development and dissemination of advanced ideas and techniques of management.

The basic premises of the Center are:

1. *The manager must continually adjust his methods* to meet the constantly evolving needs and aspirations of people.

2. *The manager's only dynamic resource is people.* If he is to get the greatest results, he must develop opportunities for each person to use his talents to the utmost and to attain satisfaction in his job.

3. *The human being has a basic need to be productive. He must feel that his work is important and that it has value to others.* People can normally attain these objectives more readily in small-sized organizations. However, since people identify themselves with their immediate associates regardless of the size of their total group, such results can be attained in large enterprises when a concern for human well-being prevails.

4. *The most effective results are achieved by organizing the work of an enterprise into rational systems and methods.*

5. *Business profits are a result of the effectiveness with which the people and other resources of a business enterprise are employed.*

The book you have just read gives you a composite description of the effective manager, illuminating the qualities of attitude and practice that lead to success in management. You have seen the types of methods that progressive managers employ in their jobs, and you have learned how they generate job satisfaction and productivity. Knowing that there is no single "Managerial Personality", you can learn to use the techniques that others have employed with outstanding results.

We trust this book has helped you understand the demands and opportunities of management as a profession. We would appreciate your comments, criticisms, suggestions and questions. As practicing managers, we are joined with you in advancing the state of the manager's art. We will give serious consideration to what you say, and we will incorporate every worthwhile idea into the body of knowledge being circulated throughout the management community.

Please use the attached form to give us your ideas. We look forward to hearing from you.

Date:_____

CREATIVE MANAGEMENT CENTER
17259 Clearview Drive
Los Gatos, California 95030

Dear Mr. Anderson:

_____

_____

_____

_____

_____

_____

_____

_____

_____

_____

Sincerely,

Name:_____

Address:_____

_____

Current Position:_____